SHERMAN TANK

A POCKET HISTORY

John Christopher

Front cover: This Sherman M4A1(76)W stands above
Utah Beach as a monument to the D-Day landings. Note
the muzzle break and also the wider tracks with HVSS.
(*Guarino*)

Title page: A British tank keeps watch on the Rhine
near Nijmegan. The additional appliqué armour patch
protecting the side sponson is clearly visible. Smoke
screens have been laid in the background.
(*J&C McCutcheon Collection*)

Opposite page: Front view of the cast hull and 75mm
gun of an M4A1 at the D-Day Museum in Portsmouth.
(*Hypermania*)

First published 2011

Amberley Publishing
The Hill, Stroud
Gloucestershire, GL5 4EP

www.amberleybooks.com

Copyright © John Christopher, 2011

The right of John Christopher to be identified as the
Author of this work has been asserted in accordance
with the Copyrights, Designs and Patents Act 1988.

British Library Cataloguing in Publication Data.
A catalogue record for this book is available from the
British Library.

ISBN 978 1 4456 0027 7

Typesetting and Origination by Amberley Publishing
Printed in Great Britain

CONTENTS

The archetypical view of a Sherman and infantrymen advancing into a village during the liberation of Europe. (*US National Archives*)

KEEP 'EM FIGHTING!

Once described as the 'worst tank that ever won the war', the Sherman tank was never going to be the equal of the German heavies, the Tiger and Panther, in a direct tank-on-tank confrontation. It was never meant to be. Instead, the Medium Tank M4, to give it its official designation, was the descendant of America's hopelessly under-gunned, pre-war designs and the product of an outmoded mind-set on the part of its military strategists. Fortunately, the Sherman's strengths lay elsewhere; in its reliability, manoeuvrability and the sheer weight of numbers produced. The Allies had more men and more tanks than Germany did and, ultimately, it was America's industrial might that out-gunned the Panzers.

At the outbreak of the Second World War in 1939, or more precisely the start of hostilities in the European theatre, the American military had only a small force of around 400 light tanks, consisting of the M1 Combat Car, later renamed as the Light Tank M1A2, and the Light Tank M2. Both of these were only equipped with machine guns originally, although the M2 was eventually beefed-up with a 37mm anti-tank gun. Developed in 1935 for the infantry branch of the US Army, the M2 featured a main turret plus side turret, an arrangement that earned it the nickname 'Mae West'. The Light Tank M3 entered service in 1941 and featured a 37mm gun in a small top turret. This vehicle should not be confused with the Medium Tank M3, which also had the 37mm gun on a top turret together with a larger calibre 75mm gun mounted in a distinctive offset sponson on one side of the hull. These were supplied to both the British and Soviet armies and it was the British who instigated the practice of naming US tanks after generals from the American Civil War to avoid confusion with their own numbering system. Thus the M3 became more famously known as the General Lee, or in a later version as the General Grant, although the 'General' was soon dropped and they became the Medium Tank M3 Lee or M3 Grant.

Intended as a stop-gap measure until a new design with a rotating turret mounting for the 75mm gun could be finalised, the M3 served the British well in the North Africa Campaign but it did suffer from a number of drawbacks. The positioning of the main gun to the side of the hull restricted the arc of fire and made the tank's profile undesirably high. Furthermore, the impact of enemy shells tended to snap the rivets, which then hurtled about the interior of the tank. Consequently, all production of the M3 ceased in 1942 once the M4 Sherman became available, although the existing M3s did see limited action in Normandy, the USSR and in the Pacific and the China-Burma-India theatre.

The design of all American tanks was in the hands of the US Ordnance Department which in turn responded to formal requirements issued by the Armored Force Board (AFB). Production decisions were governed by the Army Ground Forces (AGF) headed by Major General Lesley McNair – a dedicated artillery man with no combat experience – and it was McNair who defined the role of the Army's tanks. He cast them as infantry support weapons, a form of modern cavalry exploiting breakthroughs or softening up enemy defences. Any enemy tanks would be dealt with using anti-tank guns, either towed or in the form of self-propelled tank-destroyers. This was a deeply flawed doctrine on many levels. For a start, the tank-destroyers were basically artillery guns, lightly armoured and open-topped to minimise weight and maximise mobility. As a result they were vulnerable to attack. What's more, there simply would not be enough tank-destroyers to deal with every enemy tank encountered on the battlefield,

Christened as 'Michael' this M4A1 was the first of the Lend-Lease Shermans supplied to the British. It features the 75mm gun and, unusually, three machine guns on the hull.

Riveters assemble a Medium Tank M3 at the Chrysler Tank Arsenal. The forerunner of the M4, the rivets on the M3 had a tendency to pop and shoot around the interior when the tank was hit. (*US Library of Congress*)

The Medium Tank M3 was unusual in having its main gun mounted on a side sponson. As well as limiting the arc of fire this feature also resulted in an undesirably high profile for the tank. (*US Library of Congress*)

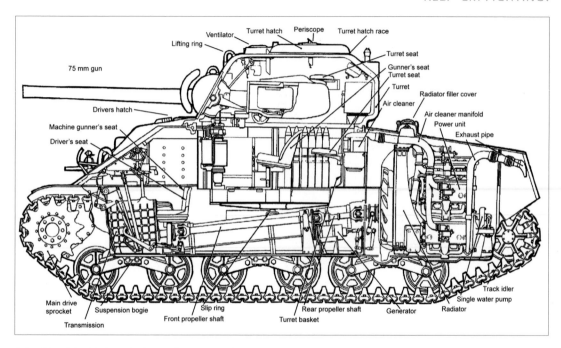

Side view of the Medium Tank M4. The engine is located at the rear with a drive shaft taking power via the transmission to the main drive sprocket at the front. Driver and co-driver/machine gunner sit at the front, with the gunner and loader in the lower turret area and the tank commander sitting at the back of the turret. (*US National Archives*)

Assembling an M4 at the Chrysler Tank Arsenal in Detroit. This is an early example with the transmission housing at the front formed from three bolted sections.

especially as McNair had expected the German tanks to act in concentrated groups while in practice they were far more scattered to avoid attack from the air.

It was against this background that in April 1941 the AFB selected the simplest of five designs submitted by the Ordnance Department for a new medium tank. Known as the T6 initially, this featured a modified M3 chassis with sloping hull and a fully rotating cast turret to house the M3 Lee's 75mm gun. This design became the M4 or Sherman tank.

At that time America had not officially entered the war, neither with Germany or Japan, but the newly re-elected president, Franklin D. Roosevelt, recognised that they had a moral obligation to support the British and Russians in their fight against the Nazis. In early 1941 he signed the Lend-Lease bill, an important piece of legislation that neatly circumventing the Neutrality Acts that forbade the sale of arms to belligerent nations. In one of his regular radio broadcasts to the nation, which he presented as a series of 'fireside chats', Roosevelt defined America's immediate role by declaring that it must become the 'Arsenal of Democracy'. By stepping up production for the Lend-Lease programme he would also put American industry on the right footing for the time when the US was fully drawn into the war as a combatant. As to when that would be was decided when the Japanese aircraft infamously attacked the US Pacific Fleet at Pearl Harbour, Hawaii, on 7 December 1941.

The first production model of the Sherman, an M4A1 with a rounded cast hull, rolled off the lines at the Lima Locomotive Works in Ohio in February 1942. Insufficient casting facilities meant that a slab-sided welded-hull version, known simply as the M4, was also developed and the manufacture of these started in July 1942 at the Pressed Steel Company in Illinois. In order to meet the President's ambitious call for

Close-up of the nose plates, complete with casting identification marks, on an M4A4 at the Imperial War Museum in London.

America's biggest tank production facility, the vast Chrysler Tank Arsenal, which was built alongside the company's car plant at Warren, a suburb of Detroit, Michigan.

the delivery of 45,000 of the tanks in 1942 alone, production was spread between several main centres. Although the US had only minimal tank-building facilities at the beginning of the war, it did benefit from a robust steel industry and an extensive railway and automotive manufacturing base. From the car industry they took the latest concepts in mass production and applied them to the building of aircraft, tanks and even the Liberty Ships, with standardised components and assembly line techniques. In addition to the Lima Locomotive Works and Pressed Steel Car Company, Shermans were also built by the Pacific Car & Foundry Company, Baldwin Locomotive Works, the American Locomotive Company, Pullman-Standard Car Manufacturing Company and, in significant numbers, by the Chrysler car company.

Chrysler used its experience of car production lines to produce the Sherman tank in vast numbers. These are early M4s with hulls of welded steel. The tank tracks are stacked in coils on the right.

This iconic image of Rosie the Riveter came to epitomise the 'can do' spirit of America's army of civilian workers which included a large number of women. (*US National Archives*)

In 1941 Chrysler constructed America's biggest tank production facility on a 113-acre site alongside its car plant at Warren, a suburb of Detroit, Michigan. Known as the Detroit Tank Arsenal it was already making Medium Tank M3s when the first of the Chrysler-built M4s was completed on 22 June 1942 and within twelve days the new tank was replacing the M3 on the assembly lines. At the peak of production the Detroit Tank Arsenal employed close to 25,000 workers, plus thousands more at sub-contractors scattered around the country. This workforce consisted of men for the most part and, taking a lead from the British, an increasing number of women. Enter Rosie the Riveter, an iconic figure celebrated in song and immortalised as the muscle-flexing, non-nonsense worker in the famous poster issued by the War Production Co-ordinating Committee. Although Rosie was in fact a riveter working on aircraft production, her 'We Can Do It!' attitude came to epitomise the determination of the six million women who took on vital war jobs, often working forty-eight hours a week, so that the men could be released for other duties. When they weren't actually building the aircraft, tanks and ships, the American public were also doing their bit to support the war effort by buying War Bonds, raising the money to 'Keep 'Em Fighting'.

In the event Roosevelt's target of 45,000 tanks for 1942 proved unrealistic and the actual output for that year was just shy of 39,000 light and medium tanks. Even so, this was an incredible achievement from what was almost a standing start. From 1941 to 1945 America's industrial might produced 40 per cent of the entire output of armaments among the combatant nations. A prodigious achievement that accounted for over 250,000 aircraft, 350 destroyers, nearly 600 Liberty ships, 200 submarines and almost 90,000 tanks. Of those tanks around two-thirds were Medium M4 Shermans or their derivatives. By comparison Germany's total wartime production of tanks was a little over half that figure at 47,000, of which around 30,000 were Panzer III and IV medium tanks, and 8,500 were the Panther or Tiger I and Tiger II heavy tanks. Incredible fighting machines in their own right, the German heavies were outnumbered by Shermans by a factor of ten-to-one. Whether the design and operational doctrine behind the Sherman tank was flawed or not, Rosie and her co-workers ensured that the Allies couldn't fail to win this numbers game.

At the Detroit Air Show the public had an opportunity to see a Chrysler-built Sherman at first hand. These displays were intended to encourage ordinary Americans to buy more war bonds.

Close-up of the later one-piece or combination gun mantle on an M4A1 with 75mm gun. The hole on the bottom right of the mantle is where the machine gun would have been, and the circular ring is one of the lifting hooks.

Above left: As depicted in this poster, the Allies' fighting machine was driven by America's industrial might which was partly financed through the purchase of war bonds. (*US National Archives*)

Above right: Final assembly shown in this patriotic image taken from Chrysler's self-promotional account of its wartime production, 'Tanks Are Mighty Fine Things'.

The Lend-Lease tanks went to a number of Allied countries, including the Soviets, and this example of an M4A2 is now in a Russian Museum. (*Yuraz*)

A stockpile of welded and cast hulls, with turrets and bogies stacked up in the background, awaiting final assembly in late 1943 at the Chrysler Tank Arsenal.

2

M4 AND M4A1

The wartime Shermans came in a range of models or types, with the main differences confined to the method of hull construction, the size of the main gun and the type of powerplant. However, there were several other minor differences and, just to confuse matters, these sometimes appeared within a particular type. In addition there were a number of major variants – the tank-destroyers, howitzers and various specialist flame-throwers, rocket-launchers, recovery vehicles, mine-clearers or detonators and others – *these are described in later chapters*. As far as the basic Sherman is concerned, the American military had designations for seven distinct production models: The M4, M4A1, M4A2, M4A3, M4A4, M4A5, which was a paper designation for the Canadian-built Ram, and the M4A6. Within these there were additional designations relating to the calibre of the main gun and method of munitions stowage, for example the M4A2(76)W was an M4A2 fitted with a 76mm gun and wet stowage system – *more on that later*. The Americans did not differentiate between the two different types of suspension used on the Sherman, although the British did. To further complicate matters the Brits had an entire naming system of their own, with the Sherman I, II and so on, including further groups or sub-categories. *See M4 Sherman Main Types for the complete breakdown.*

An M4A4 with 75mm gun, at the Imperial War Museum, London. Known by the British as the Sherman V, these had the Chrysler A57 5x6-cylinder inline petrol engine accommodated within an extended rear hull.

Detail of the standard bogie with Vertical Volute Spring Suspension (VVSS). The bogie wheels have a solid rubber tyre, and above the suspension spring bracket is a track support skid with a roller just behind it.

Chrysler promotional photo showing an M4A3(76)W with the Horizontal Volute Spring Suspension (HVSS) and the T23 turret to house the bigger gun.

Transmission housing with bolt and casting detail.

An A57 Multibank being lowered into the engine compartment at the Chrysler works. Note the extended rear hull and the straight rear hull plate, which superseded the earlier inverted horseshoe configuration.

The urgency of war meant that most changes to the design of the Sherman were either incremental or were forced by particular production issues such as the capacity to cast the tank's hull as a single unit. Accordingly, the successive designations did not necessarily indicate progressive improvements from one model to the next, or even the order in which they were manufactured, but only denoted that changes had been made. The M4 and M4A1 were identical in most details apart from upper hull construction. The M4A1 had a cast, more rounded hull, while the M4's hull was welded from sheet steel.

The suspension system on the earlier Shermans was virtually identical to that of the Medium Tank M3 with six two-wheeled, heavy-duty bogies, three on either side of the hull. Each bogie consisted of a pair of rubber-tyred wheels which were said to give a better grip in hilly terrain. Rising vertically between the bogie wheels was a bracket

Above left: An example of the Wright Continental R975 aircraft engine which was modified for use in tanks. This nine-cylinder gasoline (petrol) unit could deliver 400 hp at 2,400 rpm.

Above right: The Chrysler A57 multibank saw five six-cylinder petrol engines mounted inline. It was used on the M4A4 and derivatives including the British Firefly.

Assembly of Wright R-975 aircraft engines to be installed in the Medium Tank M3. (*US Library of Congress*)

Detail of hatch on front left-hand side of a cast-hulled M4A1. This is the driver's hatch and the slot once housed his periscope.

housing a pair of 7-inch volute suspension springs, a design known as VVSS for Vertical Volute Spring Suspension. Each bogie had a track support roller to hold the upper section of track, located above the springs on initial models and relocated above and just behind them on later tanks. The introduction of heavier guns increased the vehicle's weight and, accordingly, a new Horizontal Volute Spring Suspension (HVSS) with wider tracks was fitted instead of the VVSS.

The general layout of the Sherman tank was fairly conventional with a rear engine situated behind a firewall and connected via a shaft to the transmission, which had five forward speeds and one reverse. Engine power was transmitted to the front sprocket wheels via the controlled differential and the final drive unit had a brake system for steering the tank. The driver, sitting in the front and on the left-hand side, had two steering control levers in front of him, a gear selector to his right and clutch and accelerator pedals at his feet. The

Driver's position with the gear lever in his right hand and the two steering levers or brake controls in front of him. The co-driver/machine gunner sits to his right.

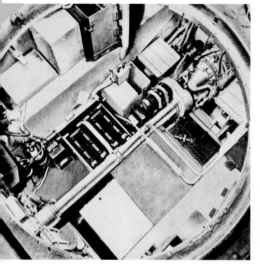 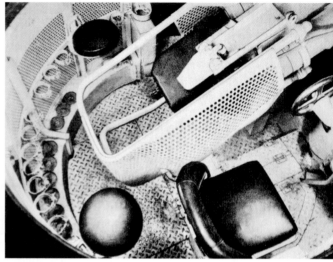

Above left: Looking down into the main turret or fighting compartment, with the turret itself and gun removed. The drive shaft runs down the centre with the transmission towards the front of the tank, shown on the right.

Above right: The turret interior with loader's seat shown at the top, commanders seat bottom left and the gunner's seat in front of the commander and on the right-hand side of the gun. The gun-elevating wheel is shown on the right. Note the ammunition racks, which encircle the turret.

driver's instrument panel was located to his left within the front of the sponson space that overhangs the tracks. The assistant co-driver/gunner sat on the right-hand side and operated the Browning .30 calibre machine gun at the front of the sloping hull.

Power for the M4 and M4A1 came from the Continental R975, a nine-cylinder air-cooled, radial gasoline engine, accessed via either a hinged top plate behind the turret, or a pair of doors at the rear of the lower hull. There was also a removable inspection plate located underneath the engine itself.

The tank's main hull consisted of a removable curved nose section covering the transmission. This originally comprised three bolted sections, although a single-piece casting was used later on. The M4A1, which was the first in production, featured the rounded cast hull, but when there was a shortage of castings the hull on the M4 was constructed from welded rolled sheet steel instead. Opinion on the relative merits of the two hull styles was divided. Some said the rounder smoother hull was better at deflecting shells, while others believed that the welded hull gave superior protection. One definite difference is that the welded hull provided more internal space. The early welded hulls had a more steeply angled front plate than later versions, with an angle of 56 degrees as opposed to 47 degrees. A third type of hull on some later versions of the M4, known as a hybrid or composite hull, consisted of a rounded cast front combined with a flat welded rear section.

Both the basic M4 and M4A1 had a cast turret. This was armed with a short-barrelled 75mm medium-velocity general-purpose gun flanked on the left-hand side by another Browning .30 calibre machine gun. Early vehicles can be distinguished by the narrower M34 combination gun mount at the front of the turret, whereas later ones were fitted with the wider and more heavily armoured M34A1 gun mount without machine gun. The turrets on the early Shermans with the 75mm gun had a flatter back without a bustle and only a single split circular top hatch on the tank commander's side. The turret could traverse a full 360 degrees and do it very quickly, which to some extent mitigated the Sherman's

Another view looking down into the forward compartment with the driver's position on the left and the co-driver/ machine gunner's to the left.

inability to pivot on the spot using its tracks. Rotation was via an electric-hydraulic drive operated by the commander or gunner, and the gunner also had a manual traversing wheel for more precise positioning.

Sitting in the highest point of the turret, on the right-hand side, was the tank commander and at his feet were the gunner to the right of the gun, and the loader to its left. In front of the gunner was the transverse hand wheel to rotate the turret and a similar vertical wheel to elevate the gun. The 75mm gun was fitted with a gyro-stabiliser system working in the vertical axis only, although it appears that gunners frequently preferred to leave it turned off as most firing was conducted from a stationary position. Aiming was by means of a periscopic sight in the early vehicles, but this was superseded with a telescopic sight by 1943. This was good up to around 3,300 feet (1,000 metres). The loader sat or stood to the left of the gun. In some respects, his was the most difficult role as he had to worm his way within the cramped space to reach the stored shells and alone among the crew he had no means of seeing outside of the tank. The turret carried up to twelve rounds of ammunition arranged around the perimeter of the turret basket, plus eight in a rack beneath the gun. There was further ammunition stowage in both sponsons and in a compartment located behind the assistant driver/gunner, giving a total of ninety-seven rounds. At least that was the official figure but there was a tendency among some of the crews to pile in as much ammunition as they could.

Unfortunately, the method of storing rounds within the side sponsons – the most vulnerable part of the tank – has given rise to a myth that the Sherman was a firetrap, especially the gasoline engined versions. They were frequently referred to by the Allied troops as 'Ronsons' because they always lit first time, and the Germans called them 'Tommy cookers'. Studies have shown that 60-80 per cent of the older Shermans did catch fire when penetrated by an enemy shell, but contrary to popular belief it was found that the gasoline fuel tanks were not to blame and that the culprit was the cordite in the tank's

Drive sprocket and track detail on the front of an M4A4 Sherman VC Firefly.

own ammunition. A partial remedy was found by welding external appliqué armour plates, 25-30 mm thick, on to the sides of the sponsons to protect the stowage bins. On later vehicles with the 76mm gun, a wet stowage system was introduced which surrounded the ammunition bins with a glycerine and water mix and this reduced the likelihood of a tank catching fire to only 10-15 per cent.

The basics of the Sherman's design and layout did not change fundamentally in the subsequent main production models:

M4A2 Differed from the M4 in having twin General Motors 6-71 inline diesels, a result of a shortage of the Continental gasoline engines. Featured a welded hull, and most of the 8,000 or so built went on Lend-Lease.

M4A3 This had a one-piece nose section, a welded hull and was powered by a 500 hp Ford GAA V8 gasoline engine. Other improvements included a vision cupola for the commander, a turret hatch for the loader and wet stowage for ammunition. Favoured by the US Army, most of these were retained by the Americans.

M4A4 Featured a three-piece bolted nose, and a welded hull, which was extended at the rear by several inches to accommodate the Chrysler A57 5x6-cylinder inline automobile engines.

M4A6 The final basic production model. Cast front, welded sides and lengthened hull, this time to house the Caterpillar RD-1820 radial diesel engine.

The process of upgrading the main gun and the consequent changes to the turret style resulted in more obvious differences among the sub-variants. The choice of weaponry and its operational effectiveness is explored in the following chapters.

3

EVOLUTION

In truth, the design of the Medium Tank M4 was already outmoded by the time it entered service. It was under-armoured and its original short-barrelled medium-velocity 75mm gun – the one taken from the Medium Tank M3 – would soon prove to be inadequate. Admittedly, it was potent enough against the Panzer II and IIIs encountered in the North African campaign in late 1943, but the Sherman's firepower failed to evolve as the war progressed and the German tanks grew more powerful and better armoured. Instead, the Allies, or at least the Americans, put their faith in the anti-tank guns and tank destroyers, blind to the prospect of opposing tanks coming into direct contact with each other. When they did meet, the M4 invariable faired worst.

During the summer of 1944 the 75mm guns were being supplemented by the 76mm gun fitted on the M4A1(76mm)W and M4A3(76mm)W. These are distinguishable by the larger T23 turret to balance the weight of the longer barrel. Firing the M62 APC ammunition, the 76mm gun could punch through 116 mm of armour at 1,650 feet (500 metres) or 106 mm at around 3,300 feet (1,000 metres). The improved High Velocity Armour Piercing (HVAP) ammo could penetrate up to 208 mm at 500 m and 175 mm at 3,300 feet (1,000 metres), although it should be noted that these figures vary with differing sources. As it turned out the 76mm gun wasn't necessarily well received by the military and it was given a lukewarm assessment in a US Army review in September 1943. While acknowledging that the 76mm gun was superior in comparison with the 75mm gun in terms of its armour penetrating power, the review questioned its overall effectiveness:

'The high explosive pitching power of the 76mm is inferior to the 75mm. The 76mm HE shell weighs 12.37lb and has a charge of .86lb explosive. The 75mm HE shell weighs 14.61 and has a charge of 1.47lb explosive. The exterior ballistics of the 76mm gun are generally less satisfactory for a general purpose Medium Tank weapon than the 75mm gun. The 76mm gun has an extremely heavy muzzle blast, such that the rate of fire when the ground is dry is controlled by the muzzle blast dust cloud.'

This muzzle blast, the shock wave emanating outwards from the end of the gun barrel, was sufficient to obscure the view of the tank commander and gunner making it extremely difficult for them to kick up dust to observe or 'sense the round' in order to adjust their aim for the next shot. The 1943 US Army review also pointed out that the 76mm ammunition occupied more storage space and, as a result, 25 per cent less ammunition could be carried in comparison with the 75mm version. It also suggested that the longer 76mm shells slowed the gun loader causing a reduction in the rate of fire. In conclusion it stated:

'If the 76mm gun is adopted for all Medium Tanks in a division then insofar as the attack of all targets except enemy armour is concerned a handicap has been imposed on the Medium Tank ... It is believed that a fairly good percentage of 76mm guns should be included in the Medium Tank unit for the purpose of giving it a sufficient share of the penetrating power available ...'

Above: The Sherman's main gun was the 75mm taken from the Medium Tank M3. It would prove to be inadequate when pitted against the German's better-armoured tanks.

Right: A column of British Shermans advance towards the German town of Goch and into western Germany. *(J&C McCutcheon collection)*

A Canadian-built Grizzley 1 at the Imperial War Museum, Duxford. Around 188 were built and these varied from the American-built tanks in minor detail only.

Close-up of the hull machine guns on the first M4A1 Lend-Lease tank. This triple gun configuration was dropped in favour of the single gun.

The Browning .30 calibre machine gun on the hull of an M4A4.

Faint praise, but the recommendation that one-third of the M4s should be armed with the 76mm gun was better than none at all, although in practice no 76mm-equipped tanks were available in time for the D-Day landings.

The American military had failed to appreciate that German tank design was not stagnant and was being continuously improved, partly to deal with the newer Russian tanks encountered on the eastern fronts. The Americans could have brought forward the development of its new heavy tank, the M26 Pershing, but this was deliberately held back so as not to interrupt the flow of Sherman M4s or their spare parts. Another factor was the delivery chain to the frontline, both in terms of shipping newly-built tanks across the Atlantic and their ability to get about in the battle-torn conditions in northern Europe. The Pershing was almost 50 per cent heavier than the M4, and the latter was small enough and light enough to be transported on regular flat-bed railway wagons or to cross the standard military girder or pontoon bridges. In

Preserved M4A3 at the US Army
Heritage Trail in Pennsylvania.
(*US Army*)

A long-barrelled British Firefly on the road to Geilenkirchen, watched by an American infantryman. (*J&C McCutcheon collection*)

contrast the Germans had the advantage that they were attempting to hold occupied territory with an established transportation infrastructure.

Just as with the gun, the thickness of the M4's armour had been determined by the anticipated efficiency of the enemy's armour-piercing ammunition, the need to keep weight down to keep the tank manoeuvrable, plus the basic doctrine behind the tank's method of operation in supporting the infantry and conducting cavalry-like breakthroughs. The armour plate at the front of the tank was 51 mm thick, about 2 inches, while on the sides it was 38 mm. On the turret the armour ranged from 76 mm at the front to 51 mm on the side, and the 89-mm-thick gun shield provided some additional protection. Later welded-hull models of the M4 had the forward armour increased to 61 mm, but even so, when Sherman met Tiger there was no contest. As one

M4A1 rear tail-light and guard, minus bulb. The bulge just beyond it is the grouser compartment vent.

Shermans of the US 784th Tank Battalion preparing to cross the Rhine, March 1945. (*US Army Signal Corps*)

A tank of the US 745th Tank Battalion rolls through Gladbach, January 1945. (*US National Archives*)

wartime tank commander stated; 'In order to take out a Tiger, I needed to hit its flanks from 60 yards (59m approx), whereas they could knock me out at 200 yards (185m approx) straight on.' A German shell could cut through the Sherman's armour plate like a 'hot knife through butter', whereas the Allied tankers would watch in dismay as their shells simply bounced off their opponents' armour.

In order to increase their own protection the Sherman crews sometimes applied additional makeshift protection to their tanks, especially to the sloping front plate. This took the form of logs, sandbags, spare track links or anything else they could find, but how effective this was in practice is debatable, although it did help to bolster the crew's moral. Weight added in this manner could have an adverse effect on the tank's performance, however, and there are suggestions that the rubber on the bogie wheels suffered greater wear.

When the Sherman went into action in northern Europe in 1944 its armour could be penetrated by most of the German tanks or anti-tank guns deployed by that time, even by the hand-held Panzerfaust anti-tank rockets, which resembled overgrown lollipop sticks launched from disposable tubes, or the more substantial Panzershrek weapon which fired fin-stabilised grenades. The official solution was the M4A3E2 'Jumbo' assault tank, which benefited from an extra 38 mm of armour plate added to the front and sides, a beefed-up differential housing at the front, plus a new heavy-weight turret protected by 153 mm of armour. Only 254 of these toughened Shermans were built and their main role was to protect the advancing columns from hidden anti-tank weapons. Initially, the Jumbos were equipped with the 75mm gun but these were later changed to the 76mm gun.

SHERMAN FIREFLY

Faced by the advances in German tank weaponry and armour the US Ordnance did consider the possibility of installing a 90mm gun on the Sherman, but this proved to be impracticable and instead

M4A3E2 'Jumbo'
with 75mm gun, at
the Army Museum in
Brussels. (*Megapixie*)

Another Sherman Jumbo, this time with the longer 76mm gun. (*US Army*)

M4A4 Sherman VC Firefly with 17 pdr gun.

the 90mm gun was fitted to the M36 tank destroyer. It was left to the British to up-gun the Sherman, although this only came about by default.

In 1943, when production of the Sherman M4 had already commenced in the USA, the Brits were working on two new tanks of their own, the Cromwell and the A30 Challenger. Both designs were felt to be superior to the 'Yank tank', but in the event several delays and a number of shortcomings revealed in the initial trials of the A30 meant that it could not be ready in time for the anticipated invasion of mainland Europe. Accordingly, the War Office approved trials with their existing 17-pounder gun, already deployed as a conventional towed gun, mounted on a Sherman chassis. Several technical obstacles had to be overcome, most notably fitting the long 17-pounder with its 40-inch recoil into the Sherman's cramped turret. This was achieved by redesigning the mechanism, shortening the recoil cylinders and positioning new ones on either side of the gun. In addition, the gun breech was modified by rotating it by 90 degrees to facilitate loading from the left side rather than from the top. A new barrel, gun mantlet and gun cradle were also devised. The 17-pounder Sherman, nicknamed as the 'Firefly' by the Brits, operated without a co-driver/machine gunner to make more space for storing the larger shells.

Officially, the Firefly was known as the 1C or 1C Hybrid, or VC, depending on the basic model of the tank so converted. 342 Sherman Fireflies were ready in time for the Normandy landings and in total around 2,000 British Shermans and a handful of Canadian Grizzlies were upgraded to Fireflies. In general they had no advantage over the conventional Shermans in terms of armour or manoeuvrability, but they did pack a bigger punch. The 17-pounder was the most powerful British gun of the war and firing standard ammunition it could penetrate 140 mm of armour at 1,650 feet (500 metres) or 131 mm at 3,300 feet (1,000 metres). In 1945, some Fireflies were fitted with launch rails on either side of the turret for 60 lb RP-3 rockets, and these tanks were referred to as 'Sherman Tulips'.

Rear view of the
Sherman VC Firefly.

The Firefly did have some drawbacks of its own. Most notably the rate of fire was lower than the conventionally-gunned Shermans, there was more kick-up of dust and dirt from the muzzle blast, plus greater muzzle flash at night, and the 17-pounder gun was too powerful for softer targets such as buildings or lightly armoured vehicles. Accordingly, the tank units were not equipped exclusively with Fireflies and they served alongside the other Shermans.

It should be noted that the US Ordnance remained uninterested when offered the 17-pounder in 1943 by the British. This was partly because the Americans were developing the HVAP ammunition, which would give their 76mm gun parity with the 17-pounder, and there were concerns that the British could not manufacture enough of the guns.

4

D-DAY TANKS

It was the largest invasion force the world had ever seen. On the night of 5 June 1944, an armada of 7,000 vessels, carrying an army of around 160,000 troops and their equipment, set sail from southern England on its way to the beaches of Normandy. Operation Overlord – the codename for the D-Day landings – was the most crucial military operation of the entire war. It was a huge gamble for the Allied commanders who relied on years of careful preparation, training and the development of the right tools to get the job done. Failure was inconceivable, while success would establish a vital bridgehead leading to the liberation of occupied Europe.

As a prelude to Overlord, in August 1942 the Allies mounted a raid against the German-held port of Dieppe on the northern coast of France. The force consisted of mainly Canadian troops plus some Brits, with air and sea support from the RAF and Royal Navy. Armoured support was provided by fifty-eight of the new Churchill tanks. The goal was to seize the port for a short period to test the landing procedures and to gather intelligence, but unfortunately the raid went badly from the beginning. Only twenty-nine of the tanks were landed on the beach. Of these, two sank in deep water and twelve others became bogged down in the shingle. Those that made it to

US soldiers pass by a Sherman at the Utah Beach Museum in Normandy. (*US DoD*)

A phantom army of rubber tanks was deployed as part of Fortitude South, the secret operation to fool the Germans into thinking that the invasion force would land at the Pas-de-Calais.

Painted on the side of a British Sherman V Crab, these markings were a visual indicator of the water's depth as the tanks waded ashore.

A Sherman V Crab pounds the ground with its flailing chains in this test run of mine clearing procedures for D-Day. The flail is at the front and the gun is facing backwards.

With skirt in its raised position, a British DD or Duplex Drive amphibious tank. This is the most complete survivor and it is part of the Bovington Tank Museum collection.

These British Valentine tanks were used for the development of the DD amphibious system and training the crews for the D-Day landings. One drawback with the Valentines was that their guns had to face backwards when the screen was erected.

the seawall were held back by a series of anti-tank obstacles and they retreated to the beach. Instead of giving Hitler a bloody nose the Dieppe raiders suffered a humiliating defeat with more than half of the 6,086 men killed, wounded or captured.

In the light of this experience the British set about devising ways of overcoming the problems encountered at Dieppe, and in 1943 Field Marshall Sir Alan Brooke appointed an armoured warfare expert, Major General Percy Hobart, to coordinate the development of specialist tanks to lead the assault on the D-Day beaches. In effect, he was tasked with creating a modern breed of siege engines, which could wade or swim ashore and negotiate the ground conditions or extensive anti-tank measures. His first task was to bring together several ideas which had already been tried, such as the Scorpion flail tanks – based on modified Matilda tanks – which had been deployed in the North African campaign, plus the mine-clearers, path-layers such as the fascine or bridge carriers, and even swimming tanks. The resulting family of weird and wonderful machines, mostly based on either the Churchill or the M4, was collectively known as 'Hobart's Funnies'.

When it came to devising a swimming tank several ideas had already been tried. These usually featured floats mounted on either side, but such a system would be too bulky for the D-Day landing craft, the LSTs (Landing Ship Tanks). In 1940, the Hungarian-born engineer Nicholas Stausser devised a flotation screen made up of waterproof canvas, which surrounded the top half of the tank and thanks to the Archimedes principle the heavy vehicle floated. In the water it would be pushed along by propellers driven by the tank's engine – hence the name Duplex Drive or DD.

In early 1944, Hobart put on a demonstration of his progeny for the Allied top brass including Montgomery and Eisenhower. These included the DD, the Crab mine-clearer which pounded the ground with its flailing chains, the Crocodile flame-thrower and assorted tank recovery vehicles devised by the engineers for a variety of roles from clearing stricken vehicles to placing pillbox-busting mines – *see*

Landing on Omaha Beach a couple of days after D-Day, this American tank has been prepared for deep water wading with barrel, mantlet and all openings sealed, plus ducts to allow air in and exhaust out of the engine compartment.

Once the area had been secured it was possibe to make more conventional and mostly dry disembarkations at Normandy. Taken in early August this photo shows an American Sherman putting ashore at Saint Martin de Varreville. (*US National Archives*)

The Sherman came to represent the Allied advance and the liberation of northern Europe, as depicted in the Overlord Embroidery at the D-Day Museum in Portsmouth.

Special Variants. Monty in particular was keen to share his new toys with his American friends and although Eisenhower was delighted with the DDs, he deferred the decision on adopting the others to General Bradley who declined the offer.

Initially the Valentine tank had been earmarked for the DD system, but in the event these were used only for training purposes as the Sherman was a more suitable candidate as a combat version. Unlike the Valentine, the Sherman's gun could face forward even with the flotation screen erected. The base of the screen was attached to the tank via a metal ring welded to the hull. The screen itself incorporated a series of metal horizontal hoops plus thirty-six inflatable vertical rubber tubes that became rigid when inflated from compressed air bottles or from an air compressor. Erected in about fifteen minutes, the screen could be quickly collapsed once the tank was on shore. The lower half of the hull was sealed to make it watertight, and the two swivelling propellers at the back of the hull were driven by a pair of powered sprocket wheels at the rear of the tracks. The DD could swim in calm waters at 4 knots, the equivalent of about 4.6 mph.

Rare wartime colour photograph of a Canadian tank crew at Vaucelles, France, in June 1944.
(*US National Archives*)

An M4A1 displayed outside the D-Day Museum in Portsmouth.

Training on the special vehicles was conducted in great secrecy. Twenty-year-old Nick Trott was a gunner on the British tanks and he recalls that the East Riding Yeomanry was the first complete regiment to be trained on the amphibious tanks. 'Initially this took place at Fritton Lake, near Lowestoft in Suffolk. The training included evacuation from a submerged tank and the use of the Davis Escape breathing apparatus which had been intended for submarines.' A tank was placed in a concrete pit and the crew waited until a torrent of cold water from two 18-inch pipes filled the pit up to 18 feet (5.5 metres) deep. In practice, the breathing gear proved effective, albeit somewhat cumbersome, and according to the regimental history 'only one life was lost' during training.

In early 1944, the East Riding Yeomanry moved to the Moray Firth, in northern Scotland, to begin a series of invasion rehearsals. Similar practice runs were carried out in other parts of the UK, including Operation Tiger, a full-scale exercise for American forces, which took place at Slapton in Devon, a site chosen because of its similarity to Utah Beach in Normandy. It was off the Devon coast, on 28 April 1944, that a convoy of nine landing craft loaded with Shermans and with combat engineers on board, was spotted and attacked by German E-boats operating out of Cherbourg. Two of the LSTs were sunk in the attack and as the remainder landed they suffered further losses when friendly fire from HMS *Hawkins*, intended to stimulate real battle conditions, showered down on the beach. As a footnote to this story, in 1984, Devon resident Ken Small recovered one of the DDs from the sea and it now stands on Slapton Beach as a memorial to the 946 American servicemen who lost their lives that fateful day forty years earlier.

When it came to the D-Day landings on 6 June 1944, the DD performed with wildly varying results. The Americans, in particular, had a disastrous time. Attempting to land at Omaha Beach were the US 741st and 743rd Tank Battalions which each had thirty-two DDs plus twenty-four other Shermans. At around 05.40 the 741st began launching their DDs even though they were still three or four miles (5-6.5 km) from the shore. The flotation system was designed to function in waves of up to 1 foot (30 cm) high, but in

July 1944: American tank crews take advantage of a momentary pause in their advance to make repairs to their M4A1 tanks. (*US National Archives*)

A Canadian Sherman in a French village, D-day +5. (*US National Archives*)

the choppy conditions they encountered waves of 6 feet (1.8 metres). Furthermore, it is thought that when the tide started pushing them away from their intended landing points many of the tank commanders, inexperienced as they were as sailors, turned their craft parallel to the shore which made them more susceptible to being swamped. Of the twenty-nine tanks launched only two made it to the beach. Some of the crews of the floundering tanks urgently radioed back to halt the launches and consequently all of the remaining tanks of both battalions were landed directly on to the beach. While most of the crewmen on the swamped tanks were rescued, at least five died. Because of this catastrophic loss of vehicles the landing force had been deprived of a significant number of its tanks, but at least the American tanks landing at the other beaches fared better with the loss of only one their tanks.

A restored Sherman rolls into the historic town of Lucca, during a re-enactment of the Allied invasion of Italy. (*US Army*)

The British had mixed results at Normandy. At Sword Beach the sea was reasonably calm and the tanks were launched about 2.5 miles (4km) out from the shore with only one tank sunk after being struck by an LCT. In another LCT the lead tank tore its screen and, along with the four tanks blocked behind it, was landed directly on the beach later on. The sea was rougher at Gold Beach and eight DDs were lost while the tanks of the Royal Dragoon Guards were launched in the shallows. Likewise, with the Canadians only half of their DD tanks were launched and of those twenty-one out of twenty-nine made it ashore.

DDs were also utilised in the amphibious landings in southern France and Italy, as well as during the Rhine and Elbe crossings in 1945.

DEEP WATER IMMERSION

One alternative to swimming is deep water wading. Protecting an M4 for short-term immersion entailed making the tank watertight. A canvas cover went over the gun shield, and the gun itself was fitted with a muzzle seal, all hatches and other openings being sealed with a special compound or grease together with sealing tape, sash cord and cloth. The engine air-intake and exhaust were covered with tall trunking or stacks mounted on special adaptors and, once on dry land, these could be jettisoned by pulling a cord which led from the turret. According to the manual a tank suitably prepared in this manner could cope with eight minutes in water up to 6 feet (1.8 metres) deep.

The Germans had also considered extreme deep water wading for tanks taking part in Operation Sealion, the intended but ultimately aborted invasion of Great Britain. A modified version of the Panzer II, a Tauchpanzer or 'dive-tank', was to have been launched a mile out and equipped with air supplied via rubber hoses and snorkels, it would have driven to the shore at a maximum depth of around 50 feet (15 metres).

5

IN COMBAT

During the drive across Europe following the Normandy landings in 1944 and until the fall of the Third Reich in May 1945, the Sherman M4 became the ubiquitous symbol of the Allies' advance in countless newsreel reports. D-Day, however, was not the first appearance of the M4 on the battlefield as it had made its combat début almost two years earlier, in October 1942, when 300 M4A1s were supplied to Montgomery's British 8th Army fighting Rommel's Afrika Korps. At the Second Battle of El Alamein, the Shermans fought alongside the Medium Tank M3 and British tanks such as the Matilda. Armed with the 75mm gun, the M4A1s were the most advanced Allied tanks on the battlefield and they successfully engaged the Panzer IIIs, which were armed with long barrelled 50mm and short barrelled 75mm guns. The British tank force outnumbered the Germans by around 1,000 to 550, almost double. The ensuing victory at El Alamein kept the Suez Canal out of the hands of the Axis powers and marked a significant turn in the tide of the war. As Winston Churchill put it, 'Before Alamein we never had a victory. After Alamein we never had a defeat.'

In November 1942, the first US Shermans saw action in Operation Torch, the joint British/American amphibious landings and invasion of French North Africa, and also during the subsequent Tunisian

An American tank rumbles through the wreckage-lined streets in the outskirts of Cologne. Sandbags have been piled up on the front plate to provide additional protection. (*J&C McCutcheon collection*)

campaign. Still fighting alongside the M3 Lees and the inadequate M3A1 Stuarts, it was in Tunisia that the M4A1 came up against the Tiger I for the first time and it proved to be a bloody initiation with heavy losses among the US armoured divisions. In the aftermath, the Americans re-organised the configuration of its tank force and by the time of Operation Husky, the invasion of Sicily in 1943, they were moving away from a tank-heavy and infantry-weak configuration to one with fewer tanks in relation to infantry. Admittedly the light tanks were being replaced by the medium M4s, but the military doctrine still cast the tank force in the role of exploiting breakthroughs. The weakness of this strategy, and the inequality between the M4 and the up-gunned German tanks and the newer German heavy tanks, became apparent the following year during the breakout from Normandy and the advance across northern Europe.

On D-Day, Nick Trott's tank, and the others of the East Riding Yeomanry, landed just to the west of Ouistreham. Despite being trained with the DDs they actually landed on the beach with ordinary Sherman M4A2s:

'We approached the beach in the morning, but they said we couldn't land yet as it was still being shelled. We eventually landed at two o'clock in the afternoon. We did pass one DD that had been blown up and there were knocked-out Churchill engineer tanks and some flail tanks still burning. We followed the railway lines into the village and parked up in the graveyard. That's when we started getting mortar shells.'

Each tank had been stocked with five days of rations and ten extra gallons of water, plus an array of wire cutters, pins for neutralising mines, and special tow ropes in case they became stuck getting to or on the beach itself. By 8.15 p.m. the tanks were moving up through Hermanville and Colville and soon encountered three long-barrelled Panzer MkIVs, which were knocked out at the cost of one of the Shermans. That night, and for many nights afterwards, there was precious little respite for the tank crews.

American Sherman on Red Beach 2, Sicily, 10 July 1943. (*US Army Signal Corps*)

Tanks being landed at Anzio Harbour in western Italy, 1944. (*US Army*)

Shermans of the French 2nd Armoured Division, on the left, alongside American tanks at Saint Martin de Varreville, August 1944. (*US National Archives*)

A Canadian tank of the Sherbrooke Fusiliers enters a French village, July 1944. (*US National Archives*)

Wright Continental R975 engine being replaced in the field, August 1944. (*US National Archive*)

'We went four days and nights without sleep – they gave us pills to keep us awake. We came up against a few German tanks, but not often and never the heavy tanks. We knocked out two of their tanks on D-Day +1, and some troop carriers, motorbikes and cars, that sort of thing. After that it was fairly quiet, but you were always on the alert waiting for something to happen. All the time you were watching.'

By the third day they were pushing towards Galmanche and beyond to Caen. The narrow tracks with high banks and tall hedges, the 'bocage', made fighting and direction finding very difficult. This terrain favoured the defenders and German anti-tank guns and Panzers were well dug-in while the Panzerfaust operators had the perfect cover from which to fire their deadly rockets. To deal with the thick hedges the Allied tank crews improvised bocage cutters, fashioned out of girders taken from anti-tank obstacles and looking like a row of teeth mounted on the front of the tanks. In many cases, the Americans put their dozer-equipped Shermans in the lead. As they continued the slow plodding advance the tanks worked alongside the infantry, taking out machine guns while the troops tackled the Panzerfaust. As Nick Trott recalls:

'We worked closely with the infantry. We guarded them and they guarded us. The biggest fear was that there was an enemy tank around the corner, or a rocket launcher behind a bush or in a ditch. On one occasion we were lead tank and we came to a sharp right-hand turn and three figures emerged from the woods and the next minute there was a phosphorous shell on the ground in front of us. The driver, without orders, reversed up the road as more bombs dropped. I fired my 75mm gun and also the turret machine gun, but I couldn't see anything.'

As the Allied tanks pushed further inland there was an increasing chance of encountering a German Tiger I or one of the new Panthers. A Sherman had no hope of dealing with either of these head on, at any range. Once hit, a Sherman's crew usually had only seconds in which to evacuate their vehicle. If the ammunition stored in the sponsons hadn't caught fire, then the gasoline probably would. One military historian, a former Sherman crewman Belton Y. Cooper, has described the M4 as a 'death trap'. America's industrial might have produced an overwhelming supply of tanks to ensure ultimate victory, but the cost in terms of lives lost was extremely high. It has been suggested that the percentage of men killed in the armoured units was higher than in any other branch of the armed services. Even so, the true testament to their bravery is that those who survived the loss of a tank in battle would get back into another one to continue the fight. 'Some had their tanks knocked out five times and still lived to tell the tale.'

As more open terrain became the norm and the supplies of HVAP increased, some semblance of balance between the opposing armoured forces was restored. It was possible for the Allied tank units to take-on the Panthers, but usually this entailed

This French M4A3, which took part in the liberation of Mulhouse, remains as a lasting reminder and as a tribute to the two crew members who were killed by a Panzerfaust. (*Remi Stosskopf*)

Shermans of the Eighth Army enter Portomaggiore in northern Italy, April 1945. (*J&C McCutcheon collection*)

A tank of the Royal Armoured Corps pushes between two blazing vehicles to make a way through for other Allied vehicles. (*J&C McCutcheon collection*)

A stricken Panther after the Battle of the Bulge. In the Ardennes Hitler had gathered together what remained of his armoured forces for one concerted push to regain territory and split the Allied forces. (*US National Archives*)

A veteran of the Battle of the Bulge, this Sherman Jumbo remains as a gate guard at the US Rose Barracks in Vilseck, Germany. (*US Army*)

Shermans of B Squadron, East Riding Yeomanry, crossing one of the numerous channels at Nederwert in the Netherlands. (*Nick Trott*)

the sacrifice of a number of the Shermans while others sought out a position from which to fire on the German's more vulnerable flanks.

The tanks of the East Riding Yeomanry were advancing to the northeast to cross the Seine at Elbeuf, one tank at a time via a Bailey Bridge, and then up through northern France to Calais and on through Belgium. For the crews their tank became their home:

'For most of the time we ate and slept in it. There was no means of heating water so it was mostly cold water and hard ship's biscuits with maybe a little porridge perhaps. If you needed the toilet you used an empty shell case and chucked it out through the hatch. When we could we slept under the tank, but they stopped that because the tanks used to sink during the night. On one occasion I woke up with my nose pressed against the underside of the tank. Fortunately I had my boots on and kicked the bottom of the tank until the co-driver woke up and moved it.'

An American Sherman burns on the streets of Leipzig in April 1945. (*US Army*)

Opposite: Soldiers of the US Army XIV Corps fighting alongside a Sherman. Most crews gave their vehicles names and this is 'Lucky Legs II'. It makes you wonder what became of Lucky Legs I? (*US Army*)

Right: A battle damaged Sherman at Iwo Jima. The wooden planking was added to protect against magnetic mines, and wire mesh covers the hatches. (*US National Archives*)

By the end of the year the tanks had reached the Ardennes where they experienced freezing conditions. The aero-engined Shermans in particular sucked the cold air in through the turret and circulated by the cooling fans it left the crew numb with cold. 'It was so damn cold', recalls Nick. 'I had to move the turret by hand as the grease froze. The infantry's rifle bolts would freeze up and they would bang them on the side of the tanks to free them up.'

It was in the Ardennes that Hitler had mustered his armoured forces for what he hoped would be a decisive counter-offensive. He believed that he could split the Anglo-American line in two and encircle the divided Allied armies in order to bring about a peace treaty in Germany's favour, thus leaving him free to concentrate on the Eastern Front. Planned in complete secrecy, the Ardennes offensive saw the German armoured division take back sixty miles of territory, inflicting heavy losses among the Allies. This 'Battle of the Bulge' was the biggest land battle of the entire war, but the German gains were unsustainable and once the weather had cleared the vastly superior Allied air-power came into its own.

After the Battle of the Bulge, General Eisenhower demanded that no more 75mm M4s should be supplied to his forces. In addition the Americans finally showed some interest in the British Fireflies and, accordingly, by the beginning of May 1945 a hundred 75mm Shermans had been converted for the US armoured units. However, none of these was supplied in time to see action by the time Nazi Germany capitulated on 8 May.

THE PACIFIC WAR

In stark contrast to the tank-led advance in the European Theatre, the nature of the Pacific War was characterised by numerous amphibious landings to capture the Japanese-held islands, and by the jungle terrain that was ill-suited to the bigger tanks. During the Guadacanal campaign in 1942, the M2A4 light tanks of the US Marines were pitched against the Type 95 Ha-Go light tanks of the Japanese

A Sherman of the 6th Division of the US Marines entering the ruins of Naha Okinawa.

Imperial Army. Both were armed with a 37mm main gun and the opposing tanks were fairly evenly matched. More advanced Japanese armour, such as the 75mm Type 3 medium tank, was held in reserve to defend the islands nearer to Japan itself in the later stages of the war, but by this time the Allied forces had replaced their light tanks with the M4 75mm. Their preferred ammunition was the General Purpose High Explosive (GPHE) shell as the armour-piercing rounds were found to pass clean through the thinly armoured Japanese tanks. Likewise, the American flame-throwers were found to be a more effective means of dealing with Japanese fortifications.

During the Second World War, Shermans were also supplied to several other armies including the French, the Free Polish and the Soviet Army on the Eastern Front which received 2,095 M4A2(76mm)Ws, plus the Chinese who got just over 800 tanks.

6

THE BIG GUNS

The US Army's doctrine of using tanks for infantry support and rapid opportunistic deployment rather than tank-on-tank confrontations, combined with the initial inadequate armament of the Shermans, created the need for a dedicated branch of anti-tank weapons. The tank-destroyers had to be fast moving, far more manoeuvrable then ordinary tanks, and were armed with more powerful guns. Greater speed came at a price, however, and accordingly they were only lightly armoured, which left them vulnerable to anti-tank fire. Furthermore, most tank-destroyers featured open-topped turrets that exposed the crews to artillery and mortar fire as well as infantry close assault.

Several of the tank-destroyers and self-propelled guns were based on the well-proven M4 Sherman chassis, and to a lesser extent on the M3, reducing the engineering and production demands to a minimum while utilising existing supplies and spare parts for maintenance or repairs. Just as with the Sherman tanks themselves, there were numerous variants with designations to indicate engine types or hull differences and, predictably, the British had their own naming system. These are the main types:

M10 TANK DESTROYER

The 3-inch Gun Motor Carriage M10, to give it its formal name, was numerically the most important of the tank-destroyers with around 6,700 built by Ford and General Motors during 1942-43. Weighing in at 29.6 tonnes, the M10 is the heaviest vehicle in this section. It is also happens to be the one that most resembles a conventional tank – complete with rotating gun turret – making it look much like a beefed-up Sherman. The main bulk of the production vehicles were based on the M4A2 chassis with the General Motors twin Diesel 6-71, and only a quarter of them used the M4A3 chassis. Above a sloping welded hull sat an angular turret with a sharply protruding rear counterweight bustle. Its main weapon was the 3-inch (76.2mm) M7 gun which fired Armour Piercing M79 shot capable of piercing 75 mm of armour at around 3,300 feet (1,000 metres), although other ammunition was carried including the infamous Armour Piercing High Explosive (APHE) which was supposed to detonate after penetration but instead had a tendency to explode upon impact. The M10's secondary weapon was a .50 calibre Browning M2HB machine gun mounted on the rear of the turret for protection against enemy aircraft and infantry attacks. The M10 had a max speed of 32 mph (52 km/h) and an operational range of 186 miles (300 km).

When the M10 was first deployed during the North Africa Campaign in 1943, its M7 gun could deal with most German tanks then in service but it frequently proved ineffective against the thicker frontal armour of the later Tigers and Panthers. Another drawback with the M10 was that its turret could move only slowly as it was hand cranked.

The M10's popular name 'Wolverine' came from the British, but this was not adopted by the Americans, who generally referred to the various Tank Destroyers generically as TDs. The British had their version, known as the 17pdr SP 'Achilles', fitted with the superior 17-pounder Mark V gun in a modified turret. This was used by British, Canadian and Polish forces in Italy and north-western Europe and can be identified by a muzzle brake and counterweight on the gun barrel.

155mm Gun Motor Carriage M40, the biggest of the Sherman-based artillery vehicles, at the Imperial War Museum Duxford.

The 3-inch Gun Motor Carriage M10 was sometimes known as the 'Wolverine'. This example, 'Bessie', is shown during the D-Day rehearsals at Slapton Sands, Devon. (*US National Archives*)

A preserved M10 photographed at the Aberdeen Proving Grounds, Maryland. The prominent bolt heads are attachment points for equipment racks or additional armour. (*Raymond Douglas Veydt*)

M36 GUN MOTOR CARRIAGE

The 90mm Gun Motor Carriage M36 was an improvement on the M10 and came into service in Europe late 1944. Christened by the British as the 'Jackson' or 'Slugger' – after the Confederate General Stonewall Jackson – the majority of M36s were based on the M4A3 with a 90mm M3 gun mounted on a new rounded turret. This was open topped, but after the war a folding armoured roof kit was developed to provide overhead protection. The M36 was exported to a number of countries after the war, including France, Yugoslavia, Serbia and Pakistan and saw action in several conflicts including the Korean War, the First Indochina War, Indo-Pakistani War, Croatian War and Bosnia. Eight ex-French M36s were later acquired by the army of the Republic of China.

M7 HOWITZER

The 105mm Howitzer Motor Carriage M7 earned its nickname, the 'Priest', thanks to its cylindrical pulpit-like gun ring. The Howitzer was intended as a self-propelled artillery gun not, as a tank-destroyer. In production from early 1942, the M7 was based on the Medium Tank M3 chassis originally, although it went on to have more commonality with the M4, including suspension. The M7B1 was fully based on the M4A3 chassis. A total of 3,490 M7s were built and a significant number went to the British under the Lend-Lease arrangement. Some had their main gun removed and these 'Defrocked Priests' were used as personnel carriers. The Canadians developed their own M7 conversion, an armoured personnel carrier known as a 'Kangaroo', a name that became generic for tanks converted to this role. M7s also took part in the Korean War.

An M10 in action in Europe. (*US National Archives*)

M10 firing near Saint Lo, June 1944. (*US National Archives*)

90mm Gun Motor Carriage M36, christened as the 'Jackson' or 'Slugger' after the Confederate General Stonewall Jackson. (*US Army*)

The 105mm Howitzer Motor Carriage M7 earned its nickname, the 'Priest', because of the pulpit-like gun ring. It is shown here in Carentan, Normandy, in June 1944. (*US National Archives*)

Preserved M7 Priest at the Aberdeen Proving Ground, Maryland. (*Yellowute*)

An M7 of the 1st Armoured Division, being unloaded at an Algerian dock, November 1942. (*US Army Signal Corps*)

The big M40 on display at the Aberdeen Proving Ground. (*Mark Pellegrini*)

M12 AND M30

The 155mm Gun Motor Carriage M12 carried a hefty 155mm M1 gun on the Medium Tank M3 chassis with Sherman bogies. Only 100 were built and they featured an open-topped area to house the gun and crew, while at the rear of the vehicle there was a spade device, much like a backward facing dozer blade, which was pushed into the earth to absorb the gun's big recoil. As there was limited space to carry the full crew of six plus additional ammunition, a gun-less version known as the Cargo Carrier M30 was produced to transport them and the two vehicles usually operated in pairs. The sole surviving example of an M12 is at the US Army Ordnance Museum in Maryland – *see Survivors*.

M40 GUN MOTOR CARRIAGE

The 155mm Gun Motor Carriage M40 was the biggest of the Sherman-based artillery vehicles. It was built on a widened and lengthened M4A3 chassis with a Continental R975 engine, plus HVSS suspension to cope with the extra weight. The gun could be elevated from 15 degrees to 55 degrees, or traverse 18 degrees to either side. The M40 had a maximum speed of 24 mph (38.5 km/h). Designed to supersede the M12 it was introduced in the final year of the Second World War and, more significantly, it also served in Korea. Post-war it was used by the British as the 155mm SP M40.

7

SPECIAL VARIANTS

Aside from the obvious variations in hull/chassis and weaponry, the Sherman provided an ideal base for a diverse range of vehicles to tackle a number of specialist tasks during the Second World War. In broad terms, these can be divided into the following categories: Amphibious landings, mine detonation, path laying, a platform for flame-throwers or rocket launchers, and armoured recovery vehicles. Just as with the M4's main types, both the Americans and the British had their own agendas resulting in a host of names and designations.

AMPHIBIOUS LANDINGS

As shown in the D-Day section the most famous of the M4 variants was the British DD, the Duplex Drive amphibious tank deployed with varying degrees of success during the Normandy landings. Despite heavy losses with the DD, the Americans continued development of a swimming Sherman in anticipation of the amphibious landings that would be required to capture the Japanese-held islands in the Pacific. In contrast to the DD with its integral flotation collar, the M19 flotation device consisted of bolt-on steel pontoons filled with rubber sponge. These encircled the tank to create what looks for all

SHERMAN TANK

Looking down on the DD amphibious Sherman, the open top to the skirt is revealed. The window in the side was added by the Tank Museum to give visitors a view of the tank inside.

The M19, America's answer to the DD, involved a 'lifebelt of steel' – flotation pontoons which could be jettisoned after coming ashore. Obviously this design is much bulkier than the DD's skirt.

the world like a miniature battleship. An official press-release issued after the end of war revealed that these 'lifebelts of steel' would be jettisoned once on dry land. 'The pontoons, a product of the Carrier Corp, of Syracuse, NY, would be released by pushing a button, which exploded rivets holding them to the tank, which continued free of its cumbersome seagoing circle.' They were first used successfully in the assault at Okinawa in the spring of 1945.

MINE DETONATION

Devising methods of dealing with mines pushed the Sherman's genetic pool to the limit resulting in an array of weird and wonderful contraptions. The US Army favoured wheeled devices such as the T1E1 Earthworm, which involved a roller unit arranged as a tricycle with three groups of armour-plate disks pushed ahead of an M32 Tank Recovery Vehicle and supported on a long boom. Developed from the similar T1 system previously devised for the M3 tank, the T1E1 was produced in 1943 and saw limited use. The T1E2 was an experimental version of the T1E1 with the number of rollers reduced to two side-by-side.

The most widely used of the US Mine Exploders was the T1E3 'Aunt Jemima' which used the same principle but with much larger 10-foot diameter steel roller disks – as tall as the tank itself – driven by chain and gearing from the front sprockets. Deployed in Normandy and Italy, the T1E3 was a hefty piece of kit and it sometimes required a second tank to help push it along. Several variations on this configuration followed with experimental vehicles using a variety of disk types and positions. Perhaps the strangest and most unwieldy of them was the T10, a design derived from an unmanned mine exploder that evolved into a manned M4 tank riding high on a tricycle of disks. The Americans also explored other techniques for dealing with mines. The T5 and T6 used angled heavy-duty dozer blades to plough their way through a minefield, while the T8 had an array of plungers carried on a frame to

The business end of a Sherman V Crab, these chains flailed the ground to detonate mines. It wasn't subtle, but it worked.

The Sherman V Crab mine-clearer, on display at the Tank Museum, Bovington.

When not dealing with mines, the Crab's flail arm could be raised out of the way. This example was photographed between Bayeux and Caen in June 1944. (*US National Archives*)

beat the ground in order to trigger the mines. Neither proved very satisfactory. Then there was the T11 fitted with six spigot mortars, which were fired ahead of the vehicle to explode mines.

The British preferred the flail technique and a series of test vehicles, known as the Sherman Scorpion, Pram, Marquis and Lobster led to the Sherman Crab which featured a rotating drum, driven from the tank's front sprocket, with forty-three chains pounding the ground. A brigade of the 79th Armoured Division was equipped with Crabs for the Normandy landings. These operated in teams of five and carried lane-marking equipment to indicate the swept lanes.

The Americans also experimented with flails and they used the Crab II, designated as the Mine Exploder T4, in small numbers. The British, in turn, dabbled with the roller method, most notably with the Centipede and Porcupine, and also produced versions of the ploughs.

PATH-LAYING

When it came to path-laying on difficult terrain it was the British who showed most interest, perhaps as a result of their experience with trench warfare in 1914-18 and also because of the shortcomings exposed in the Dieppe landings. In a direct throwback to the First World War, the Sherman Fascine Carrier transported huge bundles of wood, the fascines, ready to be dropped into a ditch to create a crossing point or in front of an obstacle to make a step. As an alternative, the Sherman Octopus featured girder ramps, which folded outwards fore and aft to cross wide ditches or gulleys. The curiously-named Sherman Twaby Ark worked in a similar fashion, while the Sherman Plymouth transported a Bailey Bridge on its back. The US Army had the equivalent in the M4 Mobile Assault Bridge.

Several American M4s were also equipped with dozer blades and hydraulic hoists, taken from the Caterpillar D-8 bulldozer, to clear a path through debris. Some versions based on the M1A1 with HVSS were fitted as turret-less dozers for the US Army Engineer Corps.

FLAME THROWERS

There were several attempts to fit a flame-thrower on the M4. These varied from the smaller E4R2-5R1 flame-guns, which were supplied in kit form to be installed in the field in place of the hull machine gun, to the M4A3R3 Flame Thrower – known as the 'Zippo' for obvious reason – which squirted a plume of flaming liquid from a barrel in place of the main gun. The British developed the Crocodile with a turret-mounted flame-thrower on a Churchill tank supplied via a towed trailer. Four M4s were also fitted as Crocodiles and supplied to the US 2nd Armoured Division in Europe. The flame-throwers provided dramatic footage for the newsreels and their main role was in attacking fortifications when conventional shelling was ineffectual. Their main drawback was short range and limited duration.

ROCKET LAUNCHERS

The T34 Calliope Rocket Launcher was developed in 1943 and consisted of an array of sixty rocket tubes on a frame mounted above the turret of a Sherman tank. The tubes traversed with the turret and could be raised or lowered via a connecting rod to the gun barrel. The name came from its resemblance to the musical steam organ which has similar pipes. The T34 saw action with the US Army in 1944-45, firing 4.6-inch or 114-mm rockets, while the T34E2 saw this calibre increased to 7.2-inch or 183 mm.

Other rocket launchers such as the T40 Whizbang were similar weapons, while the T76 and T105 had a single, large calibre, rocket tube instead of the main gun. On the T99 Multiple Rocket launcher the overhead frame was replaced by two box-like launchers mounted on either side of the turret.

TANK RECOVERY VEHICLES

The best vehicle to rescue a stricken tank is another tank, and several recovery vehicles were created by modifying the standard M4. On the American Tank Recovery Vehicle (TRV) M32 the turret and

M4A1 with dozer blade. These vehicles were essential to clear a path through the rubble-strewn streets. (*US National Archives*)

Sherman M4A3R3 flame-thrower, shooting a burst of napalm during training manoeuvres in 1953. (*US DoD*)

The T34 Calliope Rocket Launcher with its rack of sixty rocket tubes. This was linked to the gun barrel and could be elevated or transversed by the gunner. (*US Army Signal Corps*)

On the T99 Multiple Rocket launcher the overhead tubes were replaced with launchers on either side of the turret. (*US Army*)

The Beach Armoured Recovery Vehicle was a modified M4A2 with a protective superstructure and extra gear to tow or push stricken vehicles out of the way.

An American M32 Tank Recovery Vehicle with A-frame recovery gear folded back. (*Yellowute*)

gun were replaced with a fixed turret armed with a mortar to fire smoke bombs. It had a pivoting A-frame jib mounted on the front of the hull to lift vehicles, and this folded back over the length of the hull when not in operation. The M32 was armed with only the standard, hull-mounted machine gun. Further variants were based on other M4 chassis such as the M32B1 on the M4A1 cast hull chassis or the M32B2 on the M4A2 chassis. Several later versions featured the HVSS suspension system. Another modification of the M32B1 saw the removal of the A-frame and recovery gear to create the Full-Track Prime Mover M34, a heavy-duty tractor to tow artillery guns. The Tank Recovery Vehicle M32 also saw service during the Korean conflict, and a number of Sherman-based special vehicles were developed by the Israeli Defence Forces – *see Post-war Shermans.*

The British developed their own Sherman-based recovery vehicle, the Beach Armoured Recovery Vehicle (BARV); a waterproofed M4A2 featuring a distinctive, open-topped, protective superstructure in place of the turret. Operated by the Royal Electrical & Mechanical Engineers (REME), around sixty were deployed on the Normandy landings to move broken-down or swamped vehicles and to re-float landing craft stuck on the beach. The BARVs lacked the American-style A-frame and instead they either towed vehicles out of the way or pushed them aside with their wooden 'front bumper'.

8

POST-WAR SHERMANS

Although the M4 tank is thought of primarily as being a weapon of the Second World War, its work didn't end in 1945. In the ensuing decades the Sherman tank and its variants have been deployed in a number of major conflicts: The Chinese Civil War, the Indonesian National Revolution, the First Indochina War, the Arab-Israeli War, the Greek Civil War, the Korean War, the Suez Crisis, the Lebanon Crisis, the Cuban Revolution and Bay of Pigs Invasion, the Indo-Pakistani War or Second Kashmir War of 1965, the Six-Day War, the Indo-Pakistani War of 1971, the Yom Kippur War, the Tanzania-Uganda War, the Nicaraguan Revolution and the Lebanese Civil War. The main reason for the Sherman's continued presence on such a diverse spread of battlefields lies in its abundance, simplicity and standardisation of construction. Put these factors together and you had a readily available fighting vehicle plus plenty of spare parts.

At the end of the Second World War, the European theatre, and to a lesser extent the Pacific, was littered with Shermans following the rapid demobilisation of the Allies' forces. Many were left behind for scrapping, although Canada, for example, preferred to donate most of its wartime Shermans to resupply the Dutch and Belgian armies while equipping its own forces with 300 of the newer M4A2(76mm)Ws with HVSS suspension. Under the Military Aid Defense Program (MDAP) the Americans also supplied

A sea of tanks, over 900 Shermans returned to the Chrysler Tank Arsenal in Detroit for rebuilding.

tanks to several former wartime allies, most notably to France, which received 1,254 M4A1(76mm)s. Sherman M4s (76mm) also went to Japan to equip the newly-formed Self Defence Force, and also to South Korea along with the M36 90mm tank destroyer. Ironically, by the outbreak of the Korean War in the summer of 1950, the Americans unexpectedly found themselves running short of tanks to meet their MDAP commitments and numbers were made up through a modernisation programme which saw approximately 1,000 M4A1s and M4A3s up-graded from 75mm to 76mm guns. Designated as either M4A1E4(76mm) or M4A3E4(76mm) respectively, these were supplied to several countries including Yugoslavia, Denmark, Portugal and Pakistan, the latter receiving 547 of them.

For its own forces, the US preferred the newer M26 Pershing and M46 Patton heavy tanks and, at the start of the Korean War, the US Army fielded three tank battalions. These were later joined by units with the M4A3E8 – the 'Easy Eight' – with 76mm gun and HVSS, drawn from a number of sources such as the Fort Knox tank training school and the Eighth Army

The crew of an American Sherman prepare to advance along the Han River area in Korea, 1951. The fierce dragon faces were intended to scare the superstitious Chinese soldiers. (*US DoD*)

General Douglas MacCarthur inspects a Communist tank knocked-out during the landings at Inchon, Korea. (*US DoD*)

M32 recovery vehicle on the road to Hamhung during the Korean conflict, November 1950. (*US DoD*)

in Japan. By the end of 1950, more than half of the US Army's force of 1,326 tanks consisted of the M4A3E8s plus some of the bigger-gunned 105mm versions favoured by the US Marine Corps.

In combat they were pitted against the North Korean's Soviet-built T-34-85s, where they saw some fierce tank-on-tank action throughout the autumn of 1950. The M4A3E8(76mm) was well matched against the T-34-85 and both were capable of penetrating the other's armour at normal combat ranges. Despite the M4A3E8 having a smaller calibre gun it did have the advantage of the High Velocity Armour Piercing (HVAP) shell. What gave the allies the upper hand in terms of results was their superior training and considerable combat experience. As a result there were fewer head-on clashes of armour from early 1951 onwards and the Communists developed new tactics to deal with their opponents, in particular anti-tank mines which accounted for around 70 per cent of Allied tank losses – and infantry attacks carried out at close-quarters.

As the war progressed, the Shermans were relegated to second line duties as the M46 and the improved M47 Patton became increasingly available. It has been suggested that many US tank crews were disappointed with the bigger tanks; the M26, for example, had the same power-plant as the M4A3E8 but weighing 10 tons more it was far less nimble than the Sherman and it came with a reputation for being unreliable.

The Korean War, or at least the fighting, lasted for only three years and by its conclusion the US Army was phasing the Shermans out of service. In the subsequent decades the main arena for the Sherman tank transferred to other forces and to other trouble spots in the world.

ISRAELI M50 AND M51

In 1953, an Israeli delegation on a visit to France to inspect the new AMX-13 light tank was also shown the extensive stockpile of Second World War M4s. While the French tank was considered to be too

Two officers of the 18th Cavalry, Indian Army, pose in front of a destroyed Sherman during the 1965 Indo-Pakistani War. (*Abhinayrathore*)

lightly armoured, a marriage of convenience saw the AMX-13's high-velocity 75mm gun grafted on to the better-armoured hull of the Sherman and this combination became the mainstay of the Israel Defence Forces throughout the 1960s and 1970s.

In Israel, the gun was known as the M50 and subsequently the up-gunned Sherman became known as the Sherman M50. In appearance this looked similar to the Sherman Firefly as it retained the older style of turret, as used on the 75mm equipped tanks, with a counterweight at the rear. The first batch of fifty tanks featured the M4A4 welded hull, VVSS suspension and a Continental R-975 gasoline engine. The additional load on the narrow suspension resulted in generally poor off-road capability and the remainder of the M50s were based on the wider HVSS suspension and they were also re-fitted with the Cummins V-8 460hp diesel.

Around 300 M50s were in service by 1964 and these were joined by 180 M51s equipped with the more powerful French 105mm CN 105 F1 gun mounted on the later 76mm style turrets. The M51 became known by other countries as the Super Sherman, or Isherman for 'Israeli Sherman', although the Super Sherman designation was never used in Israel itself. The M50 is also sometimes referred to as a Super Sherman with the original Continental version known as the Mark I and the Cummins-engined model as the Mark II.

In 1965, the Israeli M50s first saw combat in Sinai against the Egyptian army, also equipped with its own up-gunned version of the M4 with the AMX-13 turret. Later in the 1967 Six-Day War between the Israelis and Egyptians the M50 and M51 were often pitted against Second World War-era, Soviet-built armour such as the T-34-85, although by the time of the Yom Kippur War in 1973 both sides were equipped with more modern tanks.

In addition to the M50 and M51, the Israelis developed an extensive array of Sherman-based specialist vehicles. Examples of these are displayed at the Yad la-Shiryon Museum in Latrun, which

The Israeli M50M51 with the French high-velocity 75mm gun resembles the Firefly at first glance. This is an earlier example with VVSS. It is just one of the huge collection of vehicles displayed at the Yad la-Shiryon Museum. (*Vitalyk*)

A tank crew of the Israeli Defence Force poses for a photograph during the 1973 Yom Kippur War. (*David Gal*)

Wrecked Israeli M50 photographed in 1984. (*US Army*)

A US Marine inspects an abandoned Sherman tank in Lebanon, 1983. (*US DoD*)

Israeli M32 tank recovery vehicle at the Batey ha-Osef Museum in Tel Aviv. (*deror_avi*)

The tank destroyer: M36B2 90mm Gun Motor Carriage, photographed in Croatia. (*Nicvw*)

The sea water and sands of Flamenco Beach on the island of Culebra, Puerto Rico, are gradually reclaiming this arty Sherman once used for target practice by the US Navy. (*Arenacreative*)

has the largest collection of variants to be found anywhere in the world, and also at the Batey ha-Osef Museum in Tel Aviv. These include dozers, the 'Morag', which is the Israeli equivalent of the Crab, as well as the Eyal Observation Post Vehicle, which featured a 90ft-tall hydraulic observation platform, plus assorted armoured recovery vehicles and the Ambutank medical evacuation tank. The Israeli big guns included the M10 Achilles, the M50 155mm self-propelled howitzer, and the Medium Artillery Rocket MAR-240 and MAR-290 ground-to-ground missile launchers.

By the early 1980s, the Israeli Defence Force phased out its Super Shermans and many found their way to African and Latin and South American armies. Israeli M50s were also sold to Chile where they were fitted with 60mm High Velocity Medium Support (HVMS) guns and they are usually referred to as M60s. These are said to have been the last fighting Shermans and they remained in service with the Chilean army until 1989 when they were replaced by the Leopard 1V and the AMX-30B2. It is possible that in other countries Sherman tanks were still in service after that date. Some ex-Israeli models were acquired by the Idi Amin regime in Uganda. Other users of post-war Shermans include Mexico with the M32 Chenca, plus India, Paraguay and Argentina.

There has been some interest in civilian applications for the M4. In the 1940s, Vickers produced a Sherman chassis conversion as a heavy-duty tractor for use in Africa, while the Canadian company, Morpac Industries, manufactured off-road carriers based on Sherman components.

Apart from the Russian T-34, the Sherman M4 was produced in greater numbers than any other tank in history. It may not have been the most powerful tank of the Second World War, but through its simplicity of design, dependability, ruggedness and sheer weight of numbers the ubiquitous Sherman proved itself time and time again. Today, it is rightly regarded as one of the most significant weapons of the twentieth century.

Sloping front hull plate, Sherman Firefly.

M4 SHERMAN MAIN TYPES

There were seven main M4 production models. The British had their own designations, Sherman I, II, III, etc., and also added an 'A' to indicate the 76mm version, 'B' for the 105mm Howitzer, and a 'Y' for tanks with HVSS suspension. Some changes were made during production of a given model, such as with the hull type on early and later M4s, or in some cases with the suspension.

US DESIGNATION	BRITISH DESIGNATION	MAIN ARMAMENT	HULL	ENGINE	NOTES
M4	Sherman I	75mm	Welded	Petrol Continental R975 radial	Early tanks had three-piece nose, 56-degree hull and single hatch turret. Later ones had soft-cast nose, 47-degree hull, double-hatch turret.
M4(105)	Sherman IB	105mm Howitzer			
	Sherman 1BY				HVSS suspension, wider track.
	Sherman IC Firefly	17 pdr gun			
	Sherman Hybrid I		Cast front, welded sides		

SHERMAN TANK

Looking across the engine compartment hatch at the back of this M4A1.

Rear end and engine compartment access doors of the M4A4 VC Firefly at Bovington.

US DESIGNATION	BRITISH DESIGNATION	MAIN ARMAMENT	HULL	ENGINE	NOTES
M4A1	Sherman II	75mm	Cast	Petrol Continental R975 radial	As M4 but with cast hull.
M4A1(76)W	Sherman IIA	76mm			Larger T23 turret.
M4A2	Sherman III	75mm	Welded	Diesel twin GM 6-71 inline	Most went to Lend-Lease.
M4A2(76)W	Sherman IIIA	76mm			Larger T23 turret.
	Sherman IIIAY				HVSS suspension, wider track.
M4A3	Sherman IV	75mm	Welded	Petrol, Ford GAA V8	Most retained for US use.
M4A3(76)	Sherman IVA	76mm			Larger T23 turret.
M4A3(105)	Sherman IVB	105mm Howitzer			
	Sherman IVBY				HVSS suspension, wider track

US DESIGNATION	BRITISH DESIGNATION	MAIN ARMAMENT	HULL	ENGINE	NOTES
M4A4	Sherman V	75mm	Welded	Petrol, Chrysler A57 5x6-cylinder inline	Lengthened rear hull to accommodate engine.
	Sherman VC Firefly	17 pdr gun			
M4A5					US 'paper' designation for Canadian-built Ram.
M4A6	Sherman VII	75mm	Cast front, welded sides, lengthened	Diesel, Caterpillar RD-1820 radial	Final basic model to enter production. Lengthened hull to accommodate engine. Most went to Lend-Lease.

Hull of the M4A4 Sherman VC Firefly.

Co-driver/machine gunner's periscope on the Firefly.

SURVIVORS

Sherman tanks and variants were built in such prolific numbers, almost 50,000, that there are too many survivors to list individually. This selection is only the tip of the iceberg. In the UK there are several museums worth a visit:

Tank Museum at Bovington, Dorset. Four on display including Sherman V Crab and the only DD with original floatation skirt – www.tankmuseum.org
Imperial War Museum has examples on display in London and at Duxford, Cambridgeshire – www.iwm.org.uk
D-Day Museum in Southsea, Portsmouth, has two including a BARV – www.ddaymuseum.co.uk
REME Museum of Technology, Arborfield, near Wokingham, another BARV – www.rememuseum.org.uk

Opposite: 'Michael' the first Lend-Lease M4A1 at the Tank Museum, Bovington.

Normandy has a number of D-Day-related museums and individual Shermans also crop up as monuments, often in town or village squares, throughout this region.

Musée Memorial de la Bataille de Normandy, Bayeux, includes M10 – www.mairie-bayeux.fr
Musée Août 1944, Falaise, includes M10 and M32 – www.chateau-du-tallis.com
Musée Memorial d'Omaha Beach, Saint-Laurent – www.musee-memorial-omaha.com

OTHERS WORLDWIDE

National War and Resistance Museum, Overloon, Netherlands – www.holland.com/uk/trade/coastandcountry/battlefields/warmuseum.jsp
Royal Museum of the Armed Forces, Brussels, Belgium – www.klm-mra.be
US Army Ordnance Museum, Aberdeen Proving Ground, Maryland, USA – moving to Fort Lee in 2012.
American Armoured Foundation Tank Museum, Danville, Virginia, USA –www.aaftankmuseum.com
General George Patton Museum, Fort Know, Kentucky, USA – www.generalpatton.org
Canadian War Museum, Ottawa, Ontario, Canada – www.warmuseum.ca
Royal Australian Armoured Corps Memorial and Tank Museum, Puckapunyal, Victoria, Australia – www.armytankmuseum.com.au
Armoured Corps Museum, Ahmednagar Maharastra, India, houses some interesting variants.
Yad la-Shiryon Museum in Latrun, Israel, an extensive outdoor collection of mostly post-war variants – www.yadlashiryon.com/show_item.asp?levelId=64950&itemId=2030

RECOVERED WRECKS

There are several on display, while abandoned Shermans litter many former battle zones.

Musée Des Épaves Sous-Marines Du Debarquement, Commes, France, fascinating collection of tanks recovered from the sea off the D-Day beaches, including Dozer, DD and M7.

Slapton Sands Sherman Tank Memorial, Torcross, Devon, UK, a recovered DD lost during D-Day rehearsals – www.shermantank.co.uk

M4A1 with 75mm gun, at the D-Day Museum in Portsmouth.

Chrysler publicity photograph of Sherman and friends.

FURTHER READING

Armour in Normandy – The British, Alexandre Thers (Military History Press, 2004)
British and American Tanks of World War II, Peter Chamberlain & Chris Ellis (Acro Publishing, 1975)
Churchill's Secret Weapons – The Story of Hobart's Funnies, Patrick Delaforce (Lee Cooper, 2003)
Europe Revisited – The East Riding Yeomanry of Europe and the Defeat of Germany, V.C. Ellison.
M4 (76mm) Sherman Medium Tank 1943-65, Steven J. Zaloga (Osprey, 2003)
Sherman Medium Tank 1942-45, Steven J. Zaloga (Osprey, 1993)
The Sherman Tank, Roger Ford (MBI Publishing, 1999)
Tanks Are Mighty Fine Things, (Chrysler Corporation, 1946)
US WWII M4/M4A1 Sherman Medium Tank, Editor Michael Franz (Tankogard Technical Manual Series 2005)

ACKNOWLEDGEMENTS

I would like to thank the following individuals and organisations for providing photographs and other images for this book: Abhinayrathore, Arenacreative, Chrysler, deror_avi, David Gal, Guarino, Hypermania, Campbell McCutcheon, Megapixie, Nicvw, Mark Pellegrini, Remi Stosskopf, the US Army, US Army Signal Corps, US Army Military Historic Institue, US Department of Defense, US Air Force, US Library of Congress, US National Archives, US Navy, Raymond Douglas Veydt, Vitalyk, Yellowute, Yuraz.

In addition I am grateful to Nick Trott for sharing his experiences as a Tank Gunner with a Sherman of 'B' Squadron of the East Riding Yeomanry. I must also thank Mike Gabb for additional research, and my wife, Ute, for proof reading and patience. **JC**